POEMS TO BE READ ALOUD

A Victorian Drawing Room Entertainment.

POEMS TO BE READ ALOUD

A Victorian Drawing Room Entertainment

Collected and with an introduction by
Tom Atkinson

LUATH PRESS LTD.,

Barr, Ayrshire.

For permission to reprint poems in copyright, thanks are due to the following:-

Michael Yeats, Anne Yeats and Macmillan London Ltd., for *The Lake Isle of Innisfree* by W.B. Yeats.

The Society of Authors on behalf of the copyright owner, Mrs. Iris Wise, for *Deirdre* by James Stephens.

The National Trust and Macmillan London Ltd., for *If——* by Rudyard Kipling.

The National Trust and Methuen Ltd., for *The Long Trail, Mandalay* and *Gunga Din* by Rudyard Kipling.

Feinman and Krasilovsky, P.C., Attorneys at Law, for *The Shooting of Dan McGrew* and *The Cremation of Sam McGee* by Robert Service.

Special thanks are due to the Trustees of the National Library of Scotland for permission, freely given, to reprint William Soutar's *The Tryst.*

Illustrations by
©Tony Wright

POEMS TO BE READ ALOUD

CONTENTS

A Victorian Drawing
Room Entertainment

INTRODUCTION

This little book is no more than a very personal selection of poems and doggerel.   These are the things I have long delighted to read aloud, to my long-suffering (if no longer silent) family, and to any other chance audience I have been able to catch.

They will, perhaps, appeal to others actors or preachers manque—if a more or less willing audience can be found.   The essence is the audience, and without it there is but little pleasure. Just the same, a rousing *'Dinas Fawr'* in the bathroom is not to be despised, although but a solitary satisfaction.

If it should happen that any critic-folk deign to notice this publication, they will, naturally, immediately pounce on what is *not* included.   Their favourites, their party-pieces, will perhaps not be here.   And they will castigate my choice, criticise my taste, pity my audience (as indeed I do myself).   Well, let them a' cock their snouts!   Let them all make *their* choice, and see it into print, then *I* can, and will, criticise *their* taste, *their* omissions, *their* blindness!

Of course, there is poetry of a very high order indeed included here, but there is also some fearful doggerel.   But that is the way of things.   As I say, it is not an anthology, really, just a collection, and no literary axe is being ground here.   Its only purpose is to bring together a number of pieces which well repay being read aloud —perhaps for the pleasure of a company, and certainly as a massage to the ego of the reader.

1

Anthologies are strange things, and often tell us more about the compiler than about the poets. Perhaps this collection does that, too. One anthologist, and a fine one, tried hard to be objective in his choice, but in his Introduction still had to admit, in the last analysis, the subjective nature of his choice. In his Introduction to "The Faber Book of Modern Verse", which was a most influential anthology in its day, Michael Roberts wrote that his criterion for admission to the anthology was that the poets should have written poems which "*seem to me* to add to the resources of poetry, to be likely to influence the future development of poetry and language, and to *please me* for reasons neither personal nor idiosyncratic." (Emphasis added.)

This collection is surely the exact opposite of that. These poems do no single one of the things Michael Roberts indicated, and every choice is there because it pleases me for reasons both personal and idiosyncratic. Therefore, it does not claim to be an anthology, but just a collection of things which give me pleasure, and which I hope will do the same for you, and your audiences.

Naturally, not all my poetical pleasure are to be found here. These are the ones which best lend themselves to reading aloud, and preferably with every possible vocal diapason and tremelo. Many poems, and much doggerel, is written for this purpose. Often, though, the poet is speaking directly and privately to whoever reads, and sometimes he is talking privately to himself, and sometimes again the poem is a private word in the ear of the poet's god. To read those aloud, at least in the way all this collection should be read, would be a gross intrusion on privacy, an unforgiveable eaves-dropping on a private conversation.

And yet, a word in the lug of all you fellow ham-actors. After a rumbustuous *Dan McGrew* (or *Tam O' Shanter,* if you have the tongue for it), nothing goes down better than a quiet *'Trees'.* Perhaps your toes curl or your stomach heaves at the prospect. Forget your own feelings and literary taste. You are an artist, you hold the stage, your audience will love it. And if they don't, then you have chosen the wrong audience.   Try again another day, in another place.

But if you have hit the target with *Tam O' Shanter,* then try for the bull with William Soutar's *The Tryst:-*

> *O luely, luely, cam she in,*
> *and luely she lay doun:*
> *I kent her by her caller lips*
> *and her breists sae smaa and round.*
>
> *Aa throu the nicht we spak nae word*
> *nor sindered bane frae bane:*
> *aa throu the nicht I heard her hert*
> *gang soundin wi' my ain.*
>
> *It was aboot the waukrif hour*
> *when cocks begin to craw*
> *That she smooled safely throu the mirk*
> *afore the day wad daw.*
>
> *Sae luely, luely, cam she in,*
> *Sae luely was she gan;*
> *and wi' her aa my simmer days*
> *like they had never been.*

I have very deliberately not included this most beautiful lyric in the body of the book.   It is a flower too lovely and delicate to flourish in *that* rough shrubbery!   It was written by a man totally paralysed, who lay fourteen years in his bed, and dreamed, and perhaps remembered, and then died.   He wrote in his own Scots tongue, and he, with a handful of others, show how that rough old language, despised today by so many, can express the most delicate and lovely shades of meaning.   Try translating it into standard English, and see how flat it becomes.

In effect, this little book is an attempt to stem the great rushing tide of canned entertainment. A hopeless attempt, of course. I am old enough to remember the days before radio. (And that is not so very old—the wireless did not reach every part of the country 60 years ago, even if the B.B.C. is 60 years old.) Then, families and friends made their own entertainment, and everyone had a party-piece of some kind. We all tend to think of the *ceilidh* as being something unique to the Highlands and Islands, but of course it isn't. Indeed, it would be difficult to find any part of the British Isles where the *ceilidh* is not part of folk history.

The difference between the *ceilidh* of the Highlands and Islands and those of most of the country is that in the Highlands and Islands the traditional songs and stories have been strong, resilient and long-lasting. Elsewhere, the old was driven out by the new and the corrupt, in a horrible illustration of a cultural Gresham's Law.

In my childhood, the songs sung were those of the music hall, although my father half-knew a wealth of old Border songs and ballads. He was a very accomplished melodeon player, and well remembered, as a young apprentice joiner, leading processions of lads round the Border lanes on summer evenings, him playing, and them singing. That was their pleasure and their recreation. But the songs they sang were already the songs of the music hall, although the older ballads were remembered, if not respected. Now they are forgotten, and live only in the false environment of the folk-song concerts and performances.

And that was the effect of the simple music hall. Today, the television and radio, the cassette and record, dominate all, so that the old regional differences, the old songs and stories, are assailed from another direction. The astonishing thing is that they are not finally dead.

Even in Scotland, where the tradition of home entertainment, and everyone doing their party piece has proved strongest, that tradition just manages to hobble along. I remember one very forgettable Hogmanay, when the entertainment came from the television, blaring the bonnetted inanities of Andy Stewart and the tartaned saccharinities of Moira Anderson. At Hogmanay! In the Highlands!

Still, there is a backlash. Folk (in the folk-song sense) are tiring of the mindless repetition of mindless 'lyrics', and are turning again to the old things. If you want the old ballads and the old songs, you must look elsewhere than in this book. And you don't have far to look. But if you want the sort of entertainment that kept your father and mother happy, you might well find it here.

Of course, singing, and even more, playing a piano piece, was accounted a higher form of entertainment than just 'saying a poem', but in fact no less skill— or brass neck— is required. As it happened, I took the route of the spoken word because my singing voice was guaranteed to send visiting friends and family off home very quickly. It still would, even if today respect for grey hair would demand some little applause. However, a spirited *Tam O' Shanter* or bit of Kipling can keep your audience captive, and happy, which is the reason for the exercise.

Of course, some of the items in this book are poetic drivel, if read as poems. But that is not the point. They all spring to life, all reach a new and higher level, *when they are read aloud.* It is the combination of the poem (or doggerel) with your voice, with all the art and craft you can muster, that produces the finished product and the effect you seek.

You don't have to learn the poems. Why clutter up your mind with rubbish? Of course, it is a poorly furnished mind that doesn't carry a fair stock of poetry, but surely the poems to be remembered and savoured in secret, when in love, or ill, or sad, are not the ones you want to share with an audience.

There is no reason why you should not *read* to your audience. After all, it was quite proper, in your father's day, to take your song sheets or music to a party, when "you just happened to have them with you" if you were asked to perform. You can well carry this book in your pocket, handbag or sporran. It is not conspicuous: you cannot be shamed, like the chap in the old ballad, who took his

5

harp to a party, but nobody asked him to play!

About Eskimo Nell.   She is at the end of the book, comfortable, I hope, but still hidden from children and the prurient.   She is a classical beauty, and cannot be ignored, even if there are few audiences where she can be exhibited.

Perhaps, before a furious horde of Liberated Women descend upon me, I should advance my argument that Nell is herself the very prototype of Liberated Womanhood.   Using only her own natural and highly-developed skills, she challenged and totally destroyed two of the most *machismo* characters in all of literature.   Not content with that, she verbally took the skin off their backs in a tirade full of contempt and bitterness which must have left the two even more limp and useless than Deadwood Dick's infamous masculinity.   Nell should properly be regarded as a renowned standard bearer for all women.   She ended the exploitative career of two men, not by the 'feminine wiles' beloved of romantic novelists, but by taking them on at their own game, and publicly humiliating them.

I wish I knew who wrote that epic of fornication, so that due honour could be paid,   There are many alleged to be responsible, but no-one has yet been finally and unarguably named.   That is a pity, for an anonymous masterpiece is somehow incomplete, because we cannot put it into its proper social context.   Furthermore, it allows all kinds of distortions and unauthorised versions, some of them worthy of the great original, but many trashy.   Perhaps, like the great song of the Ball of Kirriemuir, no-one actually wrote it, but it just grew and developed like some ancient folksong.   Just the same, if you can find the right audience, Eskimo Nell is guaranteed to make your name as a reciter!

So go ahead, clear your throat and transfix all talkers with a stern eye, then let it rip!

"Out of the night, which was fifty below...."

THE SHOOTING OF DAN McGREW

Robert Service.

A bunch of the boys were whooping it up in the Malamute
  saloon;
The kid that handles the music-box was hitting a jag-time
  tune;
Back of the bar, in a solo game, sat Dangerous Dan McGrew,
And watching his luck was his light-o'-love, the lady that's
  known as Lou.

When out of the night, which was fifty below, and into the din
  and the glare,
There stumbled a miner fresh from the creeks, dog-dirty, and
  loaded for bear.
He looked like a man with a foot in the grave and scarcely the
  strength of a louse,
Yet he tilted a poke of dust on the bar, and he called for drinks
  for the house.
There was none could place the stranger's face, though we
  searched ourselves for a clue;
But we drank his health, and the last to drink was Dangerous
  Dan McGrew.

There's men that somehow just grip your eyes, and hold them
  hard like a spell;
And such was he, and he looked to me like a man who had lived
  in hell;
With a face most hair, and the dreary stare of a dog whose day is
  done,
As he watered the green stuff in his glass, and the drops fell one
  by one.
Then I got to figgering who he was, and wondering what he'd
  do,
And I turned my head—and there watching him was the lady
  that's known as Lou.

His eyes went rubbering round the room, and he seemed in a
  kind of daze,
Till at last that old piano fell in the way of his wandering gaze,
The rag-time kid was having a drink; there was no one else on
  the stool,
So the stranger stumbles across the room, and flops down there
  like a fool.
In a buckskin shirt that was glazed with dirt, he sat, and I saw
  him sway;
Then he clutched the keys with his talon hands—my God! but
  that man could play.

Were you ever out in the Great Alone, when the moon was
   awful clear,
And the icy mountains hemmed you in with a silence you most
   could *hear;*
With only the howl of a timber wolf, and you camped there in
   the cold,
A half-dead thing in a stark, dead world, clean mad for the
   muck called gold;
While high overhead, green, yellow and red, the North Lights
   swept in bars?—
Then you've a hunch what the music meant ...... hunger and
   night and the stars.

And hunger not of the belly kind, that's banished with bacon
   and beans,
But the gnawing hunger of lonely men for a home and all that it
   means;
For a fireside far from the cares that are, four walls and a roof
   above;
But oh! so cramful of cosy joy, and crowned with a woman's
   love—
A woman dearer than all the world, and true as Heaven is
   true—
(God! how ghastly she looks through her rouge,—the lady
   that's known as Lou.)

Then on a sudden the music changed, so soft that you scarce
   could hear;
But you felt that your life had been looted clean of all that it
   once held dear;
That someone had stolen the woman you loved; that her love
   was a devil's lie;
That your guts were gone, and the best for you was to crawl
   away and die.
'Twas the crowning cry of a heart's despair, and it thrilled you
   through and through—
"I guess I'll make it a spread misere," said Dangerous Dan
   McGrew.

The music almost died away ... then it burst like a pent-up
   flood;
And it seemed to say,"Repay, Repay,"and my eyes were blind
   with blood.
The thought came back of an ancient wrong, and it stung like a
   frozen lash,
And the lust awoke to kill, to kill ... then the music stopped with
   a crash,
And the stranger turned, and his eyes they burned in a most
   peculiar way;

In a buckskin shirt that was glazed with dirt he sat, and I saw
   him sway;
Then his lips went in in a kind of a grin, and he spoke, and his
   voice was calm,
And "Boys," says he, "you don't know me, and none of you
   care a damn;
But I want to state, and my words are straight, and I'll bet my
   poke they're true,
That one of you is a hound of hell ...... and that one is Dan
   McGrew."

Then I ducked my head, and the lights went out, and two guns
   blazed in the dark,
And a woman screamed and the lights went up, and two men
   lay stiff and stark.
Pitched on his head, and pumped full of lead, was Dangerous
   Dan McGrew,
While the man from the creeks lay clutched to the breast of the
   lady that's known as Lou.

These are the simple facts of the case, and I guess I ought to
   know.
They say that the stranger was crazed with 'hooch', and I'm not
   denying it's so.
I'm not so wise as the lawyer guys, but strictly between us two—
The woman that kissed him—and pinched his poke—was the
   lady that's known as Lou.

Invictus

William Ernest Henley

Out of the night that covers me,
  Black as the Pit from pole to pole,
I thank whatever gods may be
  For my unconquerable soul.

In the fell clutch of circumstance
  I have not winced nor cried aloud.
Under the bludgeonings of chance
  My head is bloody, but unbowed.

Beyond this place of wrath and tears
  Looms but the Horror of the shade,
And yet the menace of the years
  Finds, and shall find, me unafraid.

It matters not how strait the gate,
  How charged with punishments the scroll.
I am the master of my fate:
  I am the captain of my soul.

THE CONGO

Vachel Lindsay

A study of the Negro Race. Being a Memorial to Ray Eldred, a Disciple missionary of the Congo River.

I. THEIR BASIC SAVAGERY

Fat black bucks in a wine-barrel room,   *A deep rolling*
Barrel-house kings, with feet unstable,   *bass.*
Sagged and reeled and pounded on the table,
Pounded on the table,
Beat an empty barrel with the handle of a broom,
Hard as they were able,
Boom, boom, BOOM,
With a silk umbrella and the handle of a broom,   *More delib-*
Boomlay, boomlay, boomlay, BOOM.   *erate.*
THEN I had religion, THEN I had a vision.   *Solemnly*
I could not turn from their revel in derision.   *chanted.*
THEN I SAW THE CONGO, CREEPING THROUGH THE
    BLACK,
CUTTING THROUGH THE FOREST WITH A GOLDEN
    TRACK.

15

Then along that riverbank
A thousand miles
Tatooed cannibals danced in files;
Then I heard the boom of the blood-lust song
And a thigh-bone beating on a tin-pan gong.
And "Blood" screamed the whistles and fifes of the warriors,
"Blood"screamed the skull-faced, lean witch doctors,
"Whirl ye the deadly voodoo rattle,   *A rapidly*
Harry the uplands,   *piling climax*
Steal all the cattle,   *of speed and*
Rattle-rattle, rattle-rattle,   *racket.*
Bing.
Boomlay, boomlay, boomlay, BOOM",
A roaring, epic, ragtime tune   *With a*
From the mouth of the Congo   *philosophical*
To the mountains of the moon.   *pause.*

★ ★ ★ ★ ★ ★ ★
Listen to the creepy proclamation,
Blown through the lairs of the forest nation,
Blown past the white ants' hill of clay,
Blown past the marsh where the butterflies play:-
                                                       All the "o"
"Be careful what you do,   *sounds very*
Or Mumbo Jumbo, God of the Congo,   *golden.*
And all of the other   *Heavy accents*
Gods of the Congo,   *very heavy.*
Mumbo Jumbo will hoodoo you,   *Light accents*
Mumbo Jumbo will hoodoo you,   *very light.*
Mumbo Jumbo will hoodoo you."   *Last line*
                                                       whispered.

II. THEIR IRREPRESSIBLE HIGH SPIRITS

Wild crapshooters with a whoop and a call
Danced the juba in their gambling hall   *Rather shrill*
And laughed fit to kill, and shook the town,   *and high.*
And guyed the policemen and laughed them down
With a boomlay, boomlay, boomlay, BOOM.
THEN I SAW THE CONGO, CREEPING THROUGH THE
    BLACK,
CUTTING THROUGH THE FOREST WITH A GOLDEN
    TRACK.
A negro fairyland swung into view,   *Read exactly as*
A minstrel river   *in first section.*
Where dreams come true.
The ebony palace soared on high   *Lay emphasis*
Through the blossoming trees to the evening sky.   *on the delicate*
The inlaid porches and casements shone   *ideas.*
With gold and ivory and elephant bone.
And the black crowd laughed till their sides were sore   *Keep*
At the baboon butler in the agate door,   *as light-footed*
And the well-known tunes of the parrot band   *as possible.*
That trilled on the bushes of that magic land.

★ ★ ★ ★ ★ ★ ★ ★
The cakewalk royalty then began
To walk for a cake that was tall as a man
To the tune of "Boomlay, boomlay, BOOM",
While the witch men laughed, with a sinister air,
And sang with the scalawags prancing there:-   *With a touch*
"Walk with care, walk with care,   *of negro dialect,*
Or Mumbo Jumbo, God of the Congo,   *and as rapidly*
And all of the other Gods of the Congo,   *as possible towards*
Mumbo Jumbo will hoodoo you.   *the end.*

17

Beware, beware, walk with care,
Boomlay, boomlay, boomlay,boom,
Boomlay, boomlay, boomlay, boom,
Boomlay, boomlay, boomlay, boom,
Boomlay, boomlay, boomlay,
BOOM."
(Oh, rare was the revel, and well worth while   *Slow, philo-*
That made those glowering witch men smile.)   *sophic, calm.*

III. THE HOPE OF THEIR RELIGION

A good old negro in the slums of the town   *Heavy bass.*
Preached at a sister for her velvet gown.   *With a literal*
Howled at a brother for his low-down ways,   *imitation of*
His prowling, guzzling, sneak-thief days.   *camp meeting*
Beat on the Bible till he wore it out   *racket and*
Starting the jubilee revival shout.   *trance.*
And some had visions, as they stood on chairs,
And sang of Jacob, and the golden stairs,
And they all repented, a thousand strong
From their stupor and savagery and sin and wrong
And slammed with their hymn books till they shook the room
With "glory, glory, glory,"
And "Boom, boom, BOOM."
THEN I SAW THE CONGO, CREEPING THROUGH THE
    BLACK,
CUTTING THROUGH THE JUNGLE WITH A GOLDEN
    TRACK.
And the gray sky opened like a new-rent veil
And showed the Apostles with their coats of mail.
In bright white steel they were seated round
And their fire-eyes watched where the Congo wound.

Redeemed were the forests, the beasts and the men,
And only the vulture dared again
By the far, lone mountains of the Moon
To cry, in silence, the Congo tune:-
"Mumbo Jumbo will hoodoo you,
Mumbo Jumbo will hoodoo you.
Mumbo..........Jumbo..........will hoodoo.........you."

Exactly as in
the first section.
Begin with terror
and power, end
with joy.

Dying down in-
to a penetrating,
terrified whisper.

"Only God can make a tree."

TREES

Joyce Kilmer

I think that I shall never see
A poem lovely as a tree.

A tree whose hungry mouth is pressed
Against the earth's sweet flowing breast;

A tree that looks at God all day,
And lifts her leafy arms to pray;

A tree that may in summer wear
A nest of robins in her hair;

Upon whose bosom snow has lain;
Who intimately lives with rain.

Poems are made by fools like me,
But only God can make a tree.

21

THE HIGHWAYMAN

Alfred Noyes

The wind was a torrent of darkness among the gusty trees,
The moon was a ghostly galleon tossed upon cloudy seas,
The road was a ribbon of moonlight over the purple moor,
And the highwayman came riding—
    Riding—riding—
The highwayman came riding, up to the old inn-door.

He'd a French cocked hat on his forehead, a bunch of lace at
 his chin,
A coat of claret velvet, and breeches of brown doe-skin;
They fitted with never a wrinkle. His boots were up to the
 thigh;
And he rode with a jewelled twinkle,
    His pistol butts a-twinkle,
His rapier hilt a-twinkle, under the jewelled sky.

Over the cobbles he clattered and clashed in the dark inn-
 yard,
And he tapped with his whip on the shutters, but all was
 locked and barred.
He whistled a tune to the window, and who should be waiting
 there,
But the landlord's black-eyed daughter,
    Bess, the landlord's daughter,
Plaiting a dark red love-knot into her long black hair.

And dark in the dark old inn-yard a stable wicket creaked,
Where Tim the ostler listened. His face was white and
    peaked.
His eyes were hollows of madness, his hair like mouldy hay,
But he loved the landlord's daughter,
            The landlord's red-lipped daughter.
Dumb as a dog he listened, and he heard the robber say—

"One kiss, my bonny sweetheart, I'm after a prize tonight,
But I shall be back with the yellow gold before the morning
    light;
Yet, if they press me sharply, and harry me through the day,
Then look for me by moonlight,
            Watch for me by moonlight,
I'll come to thee by moonlight, though hell should bar the
    way."

He rose upright in the stirrups. He scarce could reach her
    hand,
But she loosened her hair in the casement. His face burned
    like a brand.
As the black cascade of perfume came tumbling over his
    breast;
And he kissed its waves in the moonlight,
            (Oh, sweet black waves in the moonlight!)
Then he tugged at his rein in the moonlight, and galloped
    away to the West.

He did not come in the dawning.   He did not come at noon;
And out of the tawny sunset, before the rise of the moon,
When the road was a gipsy's ribbon, looping the purple moor,
A red-coat troop came marching—
                    Marching—marching—
King George's men came marching, up to the old inn-door.

They said no word to the landlord.   They drank his ale instead.
But they gagged his daughter, and bound her, to the foot of her narrow bed.
Two of them knelt at her casement, with muskets at their side!
There was death at every window:
                    And hell at one dark window;
For Bess could see, through her casement, the road that *he* would ride.

They had tied her up to attention, with many a sniggering jest.
They had bound a musket beside her, with the barrel beneath her breast!
"Now keep good watch!"and they kissed her.
She heard the dead man say—
"Look for me by moonlight;
                    Watch for me by moonlight;
I'll come to thee by moonlight, though hell should bar the way!"

She twisted her hands behind her; but all the knots held good!

She writhed her hands till her fingers were wet with sweat or blood!

They stretched and strained in the darkness, and the hours crawled by like years,

Till, now, on the stroke of midnight,

Cold, on the stroke of midnight,

The tip of one finger touched it! The trigger at last was hers!

The tip of one finger touched it. She strove no more for the rest.

Up, she stood up to attention, with the muzzle beneath her breast.

She would not risk their hearing; she would not strive again;

For the road lay bare in the moonlight;

Blank and bare in the moonlight;

And the blood of her veins, in the moonlight, throbbed to her love's refrain.

Tlot–tlot; tlot–tlot! Had they heard it? The horse-hoofs ringing clear;

Tlot–tlot, tlot–tlot, in the distance? Were they deaf that they did not hear?

Down the ribbon of moonlight, over the brow of the hill,

The highwayman came riding,

Riding, riding!

The red-coats looked to their priming. She stood up, straight and still.

Tlot–tlot, in the frosty silence! *Tlot–tlot,* in the echoing night!
Nearer he came and nearer.   Her face was like a light.
Her eyes grew wide for a moment; she drew one last deep
   breath,
Then her finger moved in the moonlight,
            Her musket shattered the moonlight.
Shattered her breast in the moonlight, and warned him—
   with her death.

He turned; he spurred to the west; he did not know who stood
Bowed, with her head o'er the musket, drenched with her
   own red blood!
Not till the dawn he heard it, and slowly blanched to hear
How Bess, the landlord's daughter,
            The landlord's black-eyed daughter,
Had watched for her love in the moonlight, and died in the
   darkness there.

Back, he spurred like a madman, shrieking a curse to the
   sky,
With the white road smoking behind him, and his rapier
   brandished high.
Blood-red were his spurs in the golden noon; wine-red was
   his velvet coat;
When they shot him down on the highway,
            Down like a dog on the highway,
And he lay in his blood on the highway, with the bunch of
   lace at his throat.

*And still of a winter's night, they say, when the wind is in the
trees,*
*When the moon is a ghostly galleon tossed upon cloudy
seas,*
*When the road is a ribbon of moonlight over the purple
moor,*
A highwaymen comes riding—
Riding—riding—
A highwayman comes riding, up to the old inn-door.

Over the cobbles he clatters and clangs in the dark inn-yard.
*And he taps with his whip on the shutters, but all is locked
and barred.*
*He whistles a tune to the window, and who should be waiting
there*
But the landlord's black-eyed daughter,
Bess, the landlord's daughter,
Plaiting a dark red love-knot into her long black hair.

Vitai Lampada

Henry Newbolt

There's a breathless hush in the Close tonight—
  Ten to make and the match to win—
A bumping pitch and a blinding light,
  An hour to play and the last man in.
And it's not for the sake of a ribboned coat,
  Or the selfish hope of a season's fame,
But his Captain's hand on his shoulder smote—
  "Play up! play up! and play the game!"

The sand of the desert is sodden red,—
  Red with the wreck of a square that broke;—
The Gatling's jammed and the Colonel dead,
  And the regiment blind with dust and smoke.
The river of death has brimmed his banks,
  And England far, and Honour, a name,
But the voice of a schoolboy rallies the ranks:
  "Play up! play up! and play the game!"

This is the word that year by year,
  While in her place the School is set,
Every one of her sons must hear,
  And none that hears it dare forget.
This they all with a joyful mind
  Bear through life like a torch in flame,
And falling fling to the host behind—
  "Play up! play up! and play the game!"

28

TAM O' SHANTER.

A Tale.

Robert Burns

"Of Brownyis and of Bogillis full is this Buke."
Gawin Douglas.

When chapmen billies leave the street,
And drouthy neibors neibors meet:
As market days are wearing late,
An' folk begin to tak the gate;
While we sit bousing at the nappy,
An' getting fou and unco happy,
We think na on the lang Scots miles,
The mosses, waters, slaps and stiles,
That lie between us and our hame,
Where sits our sulky, sullen dame,
Gathering her brows like gathering storm,
Nursing her wrath to keep it warm.

This truth fand honest Tam o' Shanter,
As he frae' Ayr ae night did canter:
(Auld Ayr, wham ne'er a town surpasses,
For honest men and bonnie lasses).

O Tam! had'st thou but been sae wise,
As taen they ain wife Kate's advice!
She tauld thee weel thou was a skellum,
A blethering, blustering drunken blellum;
That frae November till October,
Ae market day thou wasnae sober:
That ilka melder wi' the miller,
Thou sat as long as thou had siller;
That every naig was ca'd a shoe on,
The smith and thee got roaring fou on;
That at the Lord's house, even on Sunday,
Thou drank wi' Kirkton Jean till Monday.
She prophesied that, late or soon,
Thou would be found deep drowned in Doon,
Or catched wi' warlocks in the mirk,
By Alloway's auld, haunted kirk.

Ah, gentle dames, it gars me greet,
To think how mony counsels sweet,
How mony lengthened, sage advices,
The husband frae the wife despises!

But to our tale:—Ae market night,
Tam had got planted unco right,
Fast by an ingle, bleezing finely,
Wi reaming swats that drank divinely;
And at his elbow, Souter Johnnie,
His ancient, trusty, drouthy crony:
Tam lo'ed him like a very brither;
They had been fou for weeks thegither.
The night drave on wi' sangs and clatter;
And ay the ale was growing better:
The landlady and Tam grew gracious,
Wi' secret favours, sweet and precious:
The Souter tauld his queerest stories;
The landlord's laugh was ready chorus;
The crickets joined the chirping cry,
The kittlin chased her tail for joy:
The storm without might rair and rustle,
Tam didna mind the storm a whistle.

Care, mad to see a man sae happy,
E'en drowned himsel' amang the nappy.
As bees flee hame wi' lades o' treasure,
The minutes winged their way wi' pleasure:
Kings may be blest, but Tam was glorious,
O'er a' the ills o' life victorious!

But pleasures are like poppies spread:
You seize the flower, it's bloom is shed;
Or like the snowfall in the river,
A moment white—then melts for ever;
Or like the Borealis race,
That flit ere you can point their place;
Or like the rainbow's lovely form,
Evanishing amid the storm—
Nae man can tether time or tide;
The hour approaches Tam maun ride:
That hour, o' night's black arch the key-stane,
That dreary hour Tam mounts his beast in;
And sic a night he tak's the road in,
As ne'er poor sinner was abroad in.

The wind blew as 'twad blawn its last;
The rattling showers rose on the blast;
The speedy gleams the darkness swallowed;
Loud, deep, and lang the thunder bellowed:
That night, a child might understand,
The Deil had business on his hand.

Weel mounted on his grey meare Meg,
A better never lifted leg,
Tam skelpit on through dub and mire,
Despising wind, and rain, and fire;
Whiles holding fast his guid blue bonnet,
Whiles crooning o'er some auld Scots sonnet,
Whiles glowr'ing round wi' prudent cares,
Lest bogles catch him unawares:
Kirk-Alloway was drawing nigh,
Where ghaists and houlets nightly cry.

By this time he was cross the ford,
Where in the snaw the chapman smoored,
And past the birks and meikle stane,
Where drunken Charlie brak's neck-bane;
And through the whins, and by the cairn,
Where hunters fand the murdered bairn;
And near the thorn, aboon the well,
Where Mungo's mither hanged hersel'.
Before him Doon pours all his floods,
The doubling storm roars through the woods;
The lightnings flash from pole to pole;
Near and more near the thunders roll:
When, glimmering through the groaning trees,
Kirk-Alloway seemed in a bleeze,
Thro' ilka bore the beams were glancing,
And loud resounded mirth and dancing!

Inspiring bold John Barleycorn!
What dangers thou canst make us scorn!
Wi' tippenny, we fear nae evil;
Wi' usquabae, we'll face the Devil!
The swats sae reamed in Tammy's noddle,
Fair play, he cared na deils a boddle.
But Maggie stood, right sair astonished,
Till, by the heel and hand admonished,
She ventured forward on the light;
And wow! Tam saw an unco sight!

Warlocks and witches in a dance:
Nae cotillion, brent new frae France,
But hornpipes, jigs, strathspeys and reels,
Put life and mettle in their heels.
A winnock-bunker in the east,
There sat Auld Nick, in shape o' beast;
A tousie tyke, black grim and large,
To gie them music was his charge:
He screwed the pipes and gart them skirl,
Till roof and rafters a' did dirl.
Coffins stood round like open presses,
That shawed the Dead in their last dresses;
And, by some devilish cantrip sleight,
Each in its cauld hand held a light:
By which heroic Tam was able
To note upon the haly table,
A murderer's banes, in gibbet-airns;
Twa span-lang, wee, unchristened bairns;
A thief, new cutted frae a rape—
Wi' his last gasp his gab did gape;
Five tomahawks wi' bluid red-rusted;
Five scymitars wi' murder crusted;
Seven gallows pins; three hangman's whittles;
A raw o' weel-sealed Doctor's bottles;
A garter which a babe had strangled;
A knife a father's throat had mangled—
Whom his ain son o' life bereft—
The grey hairs yet stuck to the heft;
Three Lawyers' tongues, turned inside out,
Wi' lies seamed like a beggar's clout;
Three Priests' hearts, rotten, black as muck,
Lay stinking, vile in every neuk.
Wi' mair of horrible and awfu'
Which even to name would be unlawfu'.

As Tammie glowered, amazed and curious,
The mirth and fun grew fast and furious;
The piper loud and louder blew,
The dancers quick and quicker flew,
They reeled, they set, they crossed, they cleekit,
Till ilka carlin swat and reekit,
And coost her duddies to the wark,
And linkit at it in her sark!

Now Tam, O Tam! had they been queans,
A' plump and strapping in their teens!
Their sarks, instead o' creeshie flannen,
Been snaw-white seventeen-hunder linen!—
Thir breeks o' mine, my only pair,
That ance were plush, o' guid blue hair,
I wad hae gi'en them off my hurdies,
For ae blink o' the bonnie burdies!

But withered beldams, auld and droll,
Rigwoodie hags wad spean a foal,
Louping and flinging on a crummock,
I wonder did na turn thy stomach!

But Tam kend what was what fu' brawly:
There was ae winsome wench and wawly,
That night enlisted in the core,
Lang after kend on Carrick shore
(For mony a beast to dead she shot,
And perished mony a bonnie boat,
And shook baith meikle corn and bear,
And kept the countryside in fear.)
Her cutty sark, o' Paisley harn,
That as a lassie she had worn,
In longitude tho' sorely scanty,
It was her best, and she was vauntie.
Ah! little kend thy reverend grannie,
That sark she coft for her wee Nannie,
Wi twa pund Scots ('twas all her riches),
Wad ever graced a dance of witches!
But here my Muse her wing maun cour,
Sic flights are far beyond her power:
To sing how Nannie lap and flang
(A souple jade she was, and strang),
And how Tam stood like ane bewitched,
And thought his very een enriched;
Even Satan glowred, and fidged fu' fain,
And hotched and blew wi' might and main:
Till first ae caper, syne anither,
Tam tint his reason a' thegither,
And roars out: "Weel done, Cutty-Sark!"
And in an instant all was dark;
And scarcely had he Maggie rallied,
When out the hellish legion sallied.

As bees bizz out wi' angry fyke,
When plundering herds assail their byke;
As open pussie's mortal foes,
When, pop! she starts before their nose;
As eager runs the market crowd,
When "Catch the thief!" resounds aloud;
So Maggie runs, the witches follow,
Wi' mony an eldritch skreich and holow.

Ah, Tam! Ah, Tam! thou'll get they fairin'!
In hell they'll roast thee like a herrin'!
In vain thy Kate awaits thy comin'!
Kate soon will be a woefu' woman!
Now, do thy speedy utmost Meg,
And win the key-stane o' the brig;
There at them thy tail may toss,
A running stream they dare na cross!
But ere the key-stane she could make,
The fient a tail she had to shake!
For Nannie, far before the rest,
Hard upon noble Maggie prest,
And flew at Tam wi' furious ettle;
But little wist she Maggie's metal!
Ae spring brought off her master hale,
But left behind her ain grey tail:
The carlin claught her by the rump,
And left poor Maggie scarce a stump.

Now, wha this tale o' truth shall read,
Ilk man, and mother's son, take heed:
Whene'er to drink you are inclined,
Or cutty-sarks run in your mind,
Think! ye may buy the joys o'er dear:
Remember Tam o' Shanter's meare.

The Latest Decalogue

Arthur Hugh Clough

Thou shalt have one God only; who
Would be at the expense of two?
No graven images may be
Worshipped, except the currency:
Swear not at all; for, for thy curse
Thine enemy is none the worse:
At church on Sunday to attend
Will serve to keep the world thy friend:
Honour thy parents; that is, all
From whom advancement may befall:
Thou shalt not kill; but needst not strive
Officiously to keep alive:
Do not adultery commit;
Advantage rarely comes of it:
Thou shalt not steal; an empty feat,
When it's so lucrative to cheat:
Bear not false witness; let the lie
Have time on its own wings to fly:
Thou shalt not covet; but tradition
Approves all forms of competition.
The sum of all is, thou shalt love,
If any body, God above:
At any rate shall never labour
More than thyself to love thy neighbour.

THE CREMATION OF SAM McGEE

Robert Service.

There are strange things done in the midnight sun
By the men who moil for gold;
The Arctic trails have their secret tales
That would make your blood run cold;
The Northern Lights have seen queer sights,
But the queerest they ever did see
Was that night on the marge of Lake LeBarge
I cremated Sam McGee.

Now Sam McGee was from Tennessee, where the cotton blooms and blows.
Why he left his home in the South to roam 'round the Pole, God only knows.
He was always cold, but the land of gold seemed to hold him like a spell;
Though he'd often say in his homely way that "he'd sooner live in hell."
On a Christmas Day we were mushing our way over the Dawson trail.
Talk of your cold! through the parka's fold it stabbed like a driven nail.
If our eyes we'd close, then the lashes froze till sometimes we couldn't see;
It wasn't much fun, but the only one to whimper was Sam McGee.

And that very night, as we lay packed tight in our robes beneath the
snow,
And the dogs were fed, and the stars o'erhead were dancing heel
and toe,
He turned to me, and "Cap", says he, "I'll cash in this trip, I guess;
And if I do, I'm asking that you won't refuse my last request."

Well, he seemed so low that I couldn't say no; then he says with a
sort of moan:
"It's the cursed cold, and it's got right hold till I'm chilled through
to the bone.
Yet 'tain't being dead—it's my awful dread of the icy grave that
pains;
So I want you to swear that, foul or fair, you'll cremate my last
remains."

A pal's last need is a thing to heed, so I swore I would not fail;
And we started on at the streak of dawn; but God! he looked ghastly
pale.
He crouched on the sleigh, and he raved all the day of his home in
Tennessee;
And before nightfall a corpse was all that was left of Sam McGee.

There wasn't a breath in that land of death, and I hurried, horror-
driven,
With a corpse half hid that I couldn't get rid, because of a promise
given;
It was lashed to the sleigh, and it seemed to say: "You may tax your
brawn and brains,
But you promised true, and it's up to you to cremate those last
remains."

Now a promise made is a debt unpaid, and the trail has its own stern
  code.
In the days to come, though my lips were dumb, in my heart how I
  cursed that load.
In the long, long night, by the lone firelight, while the huskies round
  in a ring,
Howled out their woes to the homeless snows—O God! how I
  loathed the thing.

And every day that quiet clay seemed to heavy and heavier grow;
And on I went, though the dogs were spent and the grub was
  getting low;
The trail was bad, and I felt half mad, but I swore I would not give
  in;
And I'd often sing to the hateful thing, and it hearkened with a grin.

Till I came to the marge of Lake Lebarge, and a derelict there lay;
It was jammed in the ice, but I saw in a trice it was called the "Alice
  May."
And I looked at it, and I thought a bit, and I looked at my frozen
  chum;
Then "Here," said I, with a sudden cry, "is my cre-ma-tor-eum."

Some planks I tore from the cabin floor, and I lit the boiler
  fire,
Some coal I found that was lying around, and I heaped the fuel
  higher;
The flames just soared, and the furnace roared—such a blaze you
  seldom see;
And I burrowed a hole in the glowing coal, and I stuffed in Sam
  McGee.

Then I made a hike, for I didn't like to hear him sizzle so;
And the heavens scowled, and the huskies howled, and the wind
    began to blow.
It was icy cold, but the hot sweat rolled down my cheeks, and
    I   don't know why;
And the greasy smoke in an inky cloak went streaming down the
    sky.

I do not know how long in the snow I wrestled with grisly fear;
But the stars came out and they danced about ere again I ventured
    near;
I was sick with dread, but I bravely said: "I'll just take a peep
    inside.
I guess he's cooked, and its time I looked"; ...... then the door I
    opened wide.
And there sat Sam, looking cool and clam, in the heart of the
    furnace roar;
And he wore a smile you could see a mile, and he said: "Please
    close that door.
It's fine in here, but I greatly fear you'll let in the cold and storm—
Since I left Plumtree, down in Tennessee, it's the first time I've
    been warm."

There are strange things done in the midnight sun
By the men who moil for gold;
The Arctic trails have their secret tales
That would make your blood run cold;
The Northern Lights have seen queer sights,
But the queerest they ever did see
Was that night on the marge of Lake Lebarge
I cremated Sam McGee.

43

The Destruction Of Sennacherib

Lord Byron

The Assyrian came down like the wolf on the fold,
And his cohorts were gleaming in purple and gold;
And the sheen of their spears was like stars on the sea,
When the blue waves roll nightly on deep Galilee.

Like the leaves of the forest when Summer is green,
That host with their banners at sunset were seen;
Like the leaves of the forest when Autumn hath blown
That host on the morrow lay wither'd and strewn.

For the Angel of Death spread his wings on the blast,
And breathed in the face of the foe as he pass'd;
And the eyes of the sleepers wax'd heavy and chill,
And their hearts but once heav'd, and for ever grew still!

And there lay the steed with his nostril all wide,
But through it there roll'd not the breath of his pride;
And the foam of his gasping lay white on the turf,
And cold as the spray of the rock-beating surf.

And there lay the rider distorted and pale,
With the dew on his brow, and the rust on his mail;
And the tents were all silent, the banners alone,
The lances unlifted, the trumpet unblown.

And the widows of Ashur are loud in their wail,
And the idols are broke in the temple of Baal;
And the might of the Gentile, unsmote by the sword,
Hath melted like snow in the glance of the Lord!

Black Marigolds

(From the Sanskrit)

Even now
If I see in my soul the citron-breasted fair one
Still gold-tinted, her face like the night stars,
Drawing unto her; her body beaten about with flame,
Wounded by the flaring spear of love,
My first of all by reason of her fresh years,
Then is my heart buried alive in snow.

Even now
If my girl with lotus eyes came to me again
Weary with the dear weight of young love,
Again I would give her to these starved twins of arms
And from her mouth drink down the heavy wine,
As a reeling pirate bee in fluttered ease
Steals up the honey from the nenuphar.

Even now
If I saw her lying all wide eyes
And with collyrium the indent of her cheek
Lengthened to the bright ear and her pale side
So suffering the fever of my distance,
Then would my love for her be ropes of flowers, and night
A black-haired lover on the breasts of day.

"The pity of her slim body all broken up with
the weariness of joy.'

Even now
My eyes that hurry to see no more are painting, painting
Faces of my lost girl.   O golden rings
That tap gainst cheeks of small magnolia-leaves,
O whitest so-soft parchment where
My poor divorced lips have written excellent
Stanzas of kisses, and will write no more.

Even now
Death sends me the flickering of powdery lids
Over wild eyes and the pity of her slim body
All broken up with the weariness of joy;
The little red flowers of her breasts to be my comfort
Moving above scarves, and for my sorrow
Wet crimson lips that once I marked as mine.

Even now
They chatter her weakness through the two bazaars
Who was so strong to love me.   And small men
That buy and sell for silver being slaves
Crinkle the fat about their eyes; and yet
No Prince of the Cities of the Seas has taken her,
Leading to his grim bed.   Little lonely one,
You cling to me as a garment clings; my girl.

47

Even now
I love long black eyes that caress like silk,
Ever and ever sad and laughing eyes,
Whose lids make such sweet shadow when they close
It seems another beautiful look of hers.
I love a fresh mouth, ah, a scented mouth,
And curving hair, subtle as a smoke,
And light fingers, and laughter of green gems.

Even now
I remember that you made answer very softly,
We being one soul, your hand on my hair,
The burning memory rounding your near lips;
I have seen the princesses of Rati make love at moon fall
And then in a carpeted hall with a bright gold lamp
Lie down carelessly anywhere to sleep.

How They Brought The Good News From Ghent To Aix

Robert Browning

I sprang to the stirrup, and Joris, and he;
I galloped, Dirck galloped, we galloped all three;
'Good speed!' cried the watch, as the gate bolts undrew;
'Speed!' echoed the wall to us galloping through;
Behind shut the postern, the lights sank to rest,
And into the midnight we galloped abreast.

Not a word to each other; we kept the great pace
Neck by neck, stride by stride, never changing our place;
I turned in my saddle and made its girths tight,
Then shortened each stirrup and set the picque right,
Rebuckled the cheek-strap, chained slacker the bit,
Nor galloped less steadily Roland a whit.

'Twas moonset at starting, but while we drew near
Lokeren, the cocks crew, and twilight dawned clear.
At Boom, a great yellow star came out to see;
At Duffeld, 'twas morning as plain as could be;
And from Mecheln church steeple we heard the half-chime
So Joris broke silence with 'Yet there is time!'

At Aerschot up leaped of a sudden the sun,
And against him the cattle stood black every one,
To stare through the mist at us galloping past,
And I saw my stout galloper Roland at last,
With resolute shoulders, each butting away
The haze, as some bluff river headland its spray.

And his low head and crest, just one sharp ear bent back
For my voice, and the other pricked out on his track;
And one eye's black intelligence—ever that glance
O'er its white edge at me, his own master, askance!
And the thick heavy spume-flakes which aye and anon
His fierce lips shook upwards in galloping on.

By Haselt, Dirck groaned; and cried Joris, 'Stay spur!
Your Roos galloped bravely, the fault's not in her,
We'll remember at Aix,'—for one heard the quick wheeze
Of her chest, saw the stretched neck and staggering knees,
And sunk tail, and horrible heave of the flank
As down on her haunches she shuddered and sank.

So we were left galloping, Joris and I,
Past Looz and past Tongres, no cloud in the sky;
The broad sun above laughed a pitiless laugh,
'Neath our feet broke the brittle bright stubble like chaff;
Till over by Dalhem a dome-spire sprang white,
And 'Gallop,' gasped Joris, 'for Aix is in sight!'

'How they'll greet us!"—and all in a moment his roan
Rolled neck and croup over, lay dead as a stone;
And there was my Roland to bear the whole weight
Of the news which alone could save Aix from her fate,
With his nostrils like pits full of blood to the brim,
And with circles of red for his eye-sockets' rim.

Then I cast loose my buffcoat, each holster let fall,
Shook off both my jack-boots, let go belt and all,
Stood up in the stirrup, leaned, patted his ear,
Called my Roland his pet name, my horse without peer;
Clapped my hands, laughed and sang, any noise, bad or good,
Till at length into Aix Roland galloped and stood.

And all I remember is friends flocking round
As I sat with his head 'twixt my knees on the ground,
And no voice but was praising this Roland of mine,
As I poured down his throat our last measure of wine,
Which (the burgesses voted by common consent)
Was no more than his due who brought good news from Ghent.

Non sum qualis eram bonae sub regno Cynarae

Ernest Dowson

Last night, ah, yesternight, betwixt her lips and mine
There fell thy shadow, Cynara! thy breath was shed
Upon my soul between the kisses and the wine;
And I was desolate and sick of an old passion,
*　　　Yea, I was desolate and bowed my head:*
I have been faithful to thee, Cynara! in my fashion.

All night upon mine heart I felt her warm heart beat,
Night-long within mine arms in love and sleep she lay;
Surely the kisses of her bought red mouth were sweet;
But I was desolate and sick of an old passion,
*　　　When I awoke and found the dawn was gray:*
I have been faithful to thee, Cynara! in my fashion.

I have forgot much, Cynara! gone with the wind,
Flung roses, roses, riotously with the throng,
Dancing, to put thy pale lost lilies out of mind;
But I was desolate and sick of an old passion,
*　　　Yea, all the time, because the dance was long:*
I have been faithful to thee, Cynara! in my fashion.

I cried for madder music and for stronger wine,
But when the feast is finished and the lamps expire,
Then falls thy shadow, Cynara! the night is thine;
And I am desolate and sick of an old passion,
*　　　Yea, hungry for the lips of my desire:*
I have been faithful to thee, Cynara! in my fashion.

HOLY WILLIE'S PRAYER

Robert Burns.

O THOU, who in the heavens does dwell,
Who, as it pleases best Thysel,
Sends ane to heaven an' ten to hell,
   A' for thy glory,
And no for ony gude or ill
    They've done afore Thee!

I bless and praise Thy matchlesss might,
When thousands Thou has left in night,
That I am here afore Thy sight,
   For gifts an' grace
A burning and a shining light
    To a' this place.

What was I, or my generation,
That I should get sic exaltation,
I, wha deserve most just damnation
   For broken laws,
Five thousand years ere my creation,
    Thro' Adam's cause.

When frae my mither's womb I fell,
Thou might hae plunged me in hell,
To gnash my gums, to weep and wail,
   In burnin' lakes,
Where damned devils roar and yell,
    Chain'd to their stakes.

Yet I am here, a chosen sample,
To show thy grace is great and ample;
I'm here a pillar o' Thy temple,
    Strong as a rock,
A guide, a buckler, and example
    To a' thy flock.

O Lord, Thou kens what zeal I bear,
When drinkers drink, an' swearers swear,
An' singin' there, an' dancin' here,
    Wi' great and sma';
For I am keepit by Thy fear
    Free frae them a'.

But yet, O Lord! confess I must,
At times I'm fashed wi' fleshly lust:
An' sometimes, too, in warldly trust,
    Vile self gets in;
But Thou remembers we are dust,
    Defil'd wi' sin.

O Lord! yestreen, Thou kens, wi' Meg—
Thy pardon I sincerely beg,
O! may't ne'er be a livin' plague
    To my dishonour,
An' I'll ne'er lift a lawless leg
    Again upon her.

Besides, I farther maun allow,
Wi' Leezie's lass three times I trow—
But Lord, that Friday I was fou,
    When I cam near her;
Or else, Thou kens, Thy servant true
    Wad never steer her.

Maybe Thou lets this fleshly thorn
Buffet Thy servant e'en an' morn,
Lest he owre proud and high should turn
　　　That he's sae gifted:
If sae, Thy han' maun e'en be borne,
　　　Until Thou lift it.

Lord, bless Thy chosen in the place,
For here thou hast a chosen race:
But God confound their stubborn face
　　　An' blast their name,
Wha brings Thy elders to disgrace
　　　An' public shame.

Lord, mind Gaw'n Hamilton's deserts;
He drinks, an' swears, an' plays at carts,
Yet has sae mony takin' arts,
　　　Wi' great an' sma',
Frae God's ain priest the people's hearts
　　　He steals awa.

An' when we chastened him therefor,
Thou kens how he bred sic a splore,
An' set the warld in a roar
　　　O' laughin' at us;—
Curse Thou his basket and his store,
　　　Kail an' potatoes!

Lord, hear my earnest cry and pray'r,
Against that Presbyt'ry o' Ayr;
Thy strong right hand, Lord, make it bare
　　　Upo' their heads;
Lord visit them, an' dinna spare,
　　　For their misdeeds.

O Lord, my God! that glib-tongued Aiken,
My vera heart an' flesh are quakin'
To think how we stood sweatin' shakin',
  An' pissed wi' dread,
While he, wi' hingin' lip an' snakin'
  Held up his head.

Lord, in Thy day o' vengeance try him,
Lord, visit them wha did employ him,
And pass not in Thy mercy by them,
  Nor hear their pray'rs,
But for Thy people's sake destroy them,
  An' dinna spare.

But, Lord, remember me an' mine
Wi' mercies temporal an' divine,
That I for grace an' gear may shine,
  Excell'd by nane,
And a' the glory shall be thine,
  Amen, Amen!

THE LONG TRAIL

Rudyard Kipling

There's a whisper down the field where the year has shot
her yield,
  And the ricks stand grey to the sun,
Singing: "Over, then, come over, for the bee has quit the
clover,
  "And your English summer's done,"

   You have heard the beat of the off-shore wind,
   And the thresh of the deep-sea rain;
   You have heard the song—how long? how long ?
   Pull out on the trail again!
Ha' done with the Tents of Shem, dear lass,
We've seen the seasons through,
And it's time to turn on the old trail, our own trail, the
out trail,
Pull out, pull out, on the Long Trail—the trail that is
always new!
It's North you may run to the rime-ringed sun
  Or South to the blind Horn's hate;
Or East all the way into Mississippi Bay,
  Or West to the Golden Gate—
   Where the blindest bluffs hold good, dear lass,
   And the wildest tales are true,
   And the men bulk big on the old trail, our own trail,
     the out trail,
   And life runs large on the Long Trail—the trail that
     is always new.

57

"The Long Trail — the trail that is always new."

The days are sick and cold, and the skies are grey and
      old,
  And the twice-breathed airs blow damp;
And I'd sell my tired soul for the bucking beam-sea roll
  Of a black Bilbao tramp,
      With her load-line over her hatch, dear lass,
      And a drunken Dago crew,
      And her nose held down on the old trail, our own
        trail, the out trail,
      From Cadiz south on the Long Trail—the trail that is
        always new.

There be triple ways to take, of the eagle or the snake,
  Or the way of a man with a maid;
But the sweetest way to me is a ship's upon the sea
  In the heel of the North-East Trade.
      Can you hear the crash on her bows, dear lass,
      And the drum of the racing screw,
      As she ships it green on the old trail, our own trail,
        the out trail,
      As she lifts and 'scends on the Long Trail—the trail
        that is always new.

See the shaking funnels roar, with the Peter at the fore,
  And the fenders grind and heave,
And the derricks clack and grate, as the tackle hooks the
      crate,
  And the fall-rope whines through the sheave;
      It's "Gang-plank up and in." dear lass,
      It's "Hawsers warp her through!"
      And it's "All clear aft" on the old trail, our own trail,
        the out trail,
      We're backing down on the Long Trail—the trail
        that is always new.

O the mutter overside, when the port-fog holds us tied,
  And the sirens hoot their dread,
When foot by foot we creep o'er the hueless, viewless
      deep,
   To the sob of the questing lead!
      It's down by the Lower Hope, dear lass,
      With the Gunfleet Sands in view,
      Till the Mouse swings green on the old trail, our own
        trail, the out trail,
      And the Gull Light lifts on the Long Trail—the trail
        that is always new.

O the blazing tropic night, when the wake's a welt of light
  That holds the hot sky tame.
And the steady fore-foot snores through the planet-
    powdered floors
  Where the scared whale flukes in flame!
      Her plates are flaked by the sun, dear lass,
      And her ropes are taut with the dew,
      For we're booming down on the old trail, our own
        trail, the out trail,
      We're sagging south on the Long Trail—the trail
        that is always new.

Then home, get her home, where the drunken rollers
    comb,
  And the shouting seas drive by,
And the engines stamp and ring, and the wet bows reel
    and swing,
  And the Southern Cross rides high!
      Yes, the old lost stars wheel back, dear lass,
      That blaze in the velvet blue.
      They're all old friends on the old trail, our own trail,
          the out trail,
      They're God's own guides on the Long Trail—the
          trail that is always new.

Fly forward, O my heart, from the Foreland to the Start—
  We're steaming all too slow,
And it's twenty thousand mile to our little lazy isle
  Where the trumpet-orchids blow!
      You have heard the call of the off-shore wind
      And the voice of the deep-sea rain;
      You have heard the song—how long?—how long?
      Pull out on the trail again!

The Lord knows what we may find, dear lass,
And the Deuce knows what we may do—
But we're back once more on the old trail, our own trail,
    the out trail,
We're down, hull-down, on the Long Trail— the trail that
    is always new!

To A Mouse

(On turning her up in her nest with the plow, November 1785)

Robert Burns

Wee, sleekit, cow'rin' tim'rous beastie,
Oh, what a panic's in thy breastie!
Thou needs na start awa sae hasty
    Wi' bickerin' brattle!
I wad be laith to rin an' chase thee
    Wi' murderin' pattle!

I'm truly sorry man's dominion
Has broken nature's social union
An' justifies that ill opinion
    Which makes thee startle
At me, thy poor earthborn companion
    An' fellow mortal!

I doubt na, whyles, but thou may thieve;
What then? poor beastie, thou maun live!
A daimen icker in a thrave
    'S a sma' request;
I'll get a blessin' wi' the lave,
    An' never miss't!

Thy wee bit housie, too, in ruin!
Its silly wa's the wind's are strewin'.
An' naething now to big a new ane
    O' foggage green;
An' bleak December's win's ensuin',
    Baith snell an' keen!

Thou saw the fields laid bare an' waste.
An' weary winter comin' fast,
An' cozy here beneath the blast
   Thou thought to dwell—
Till crash! the cruel colter passed
   Out through thy cell.

That wee bit heap o' leaves an' stibble
Has cost thee mony a weary nibble!
Now thou's turned out, for a' thy trouble,
   But house or hald,
To thole the winter's sleety dribble
   An' crancreuch cauld!

But, Mousie, thou are no thy lane
In proving foresight may be vain;
The best-laid schemes o' mice an' men
   Gang aft agley
An' lea'e us naught but grief an' pain
   For promised joy.

Still, thou art blest, compared wi' me!
The present only toucheth thee;
But och! I backward cast my e'e
   On prospects drear!
An' forward, though I canna see,
   I guess an' fear.

JABBERWOCKY

Lewis Carroll

'Twas brillig, and the slithy toves
  Did gyre and gimble in the wabe;
All mimsy were the borogoves,
  And the mome raths outgrabe.

"Beware the Jabberwock, my son!
  The jaws that bite, the claws that catch!
Beware the Jubjub bird, and shun
  The frumious Bandersnatch!"

He took his vorpal sword in hand:
  Long time the manxome foe he sought,—
So rested he by the Tumtum tree,
  And stood awhile in thought.

And as in uffish thought he stood,
  The Jabberwock, with eyes of flame,
Came whiffling through the tulgey wood,
  And burbled as it came!

One, two! One, two! And through and through
  The vorpal blade went snicker-snack!
He left it dead, and with its head
  He went galumphing back.

"And hast thou slain the Jabberwock?
　　Come to my arms, my beamish boy!
O frabjous day! Callooh! Callay!"
　　He chortled in his joy.

'Twas brillig, and the slithy toves
　　Did gyre and gimble in the wabe;
All mimsy were the borogoves,
　　And the mome raths outgrabe.

The Song Of The Shirt

Thomas Hood

With fingers weary and worn,
  With eyelids heavy and red,
A woman sat, in unwomanly rags,
  Plying her needle and thread —
          Stitch! stitch! stitch!
In poverty, hunger and dirt,
  And still with a voice of dolorous pitch
She sang the 'Song of the Shirt'.

          'Work! work! work!
While the cock is crowing aloof!
          And work — work —work,
Till the stars shine through the roof!!
It's oh! to be a slave
  Along with the barbarous Turk,
Where a woman has never a soul to save,
  If this is Christian work!

          'Work — work —work
Till the brain begins to swim;
          Work — work — work
Till the eyes are heavy and dim!
Seam and gusset and band,
  Band and gusset and seam,
Till over the buttons I fall asleep,
  And sew them on in a dream!

'Oh, Men with Sisters dear!
  Oh, Men with Mothers and Wives!
It is not linen you're wearing out,
  But human creatures's lives!
                Stitch — stitch — stitch,
  In poverty, hunger and dirt,
Sewing at once, with a double thread,
  A Shroud as well as a Shirt!

'But why do I talk of Death?
  That Phantom of grisly bone,
I hardly fear its terrible shape,
  It seems so like my own —
  It seems so like my own,
Because of the fasts I keep;
Oh, God! that bread should be so dear,
  And flesh and blood so cheap!

'Work — work — work!
  My labour never flags;
And what are its wages? A bed of straw,
  A crust of bread — and rags.
That shatter'd roof — and this naked floor —
  A table — a broken chair —
And a wall so blank, my shadow I thank
  For sometimes falling there!

'Work — work — work!
From weary chime to chime,
  Work — work — work —
As prisoners work for crime!
  Band and gusset and seam,
Seam and gusset and band,
Till the heart is sick, and the brain benumbd'd,
  As well as the weary hand.

'Work — work — work,
In the dull December light,
  And work — work — work,
When the weather is warm and bright —
While underneath the eaves
  The brooding swallows cling
As if to show me their sunny backs
  And twit me with the spring.

'Oh! but to breathe the breath
Of the cowslip and primrose sweet —
  With the sky above my head,
And the grass beneath my feet,
For only one short hour
  To feel as I used to feel,
Before I knew the woes of want
  And the walk that costs a meal!

'Oh! but for one short hour!
   A respite however brief!
No blessed leisure for Love or Hope,
   But only time for Grief!
A little weeping would ease my heart,
But in their briny bed
My tears must stop, for every drop
   Hinders needle and thread!'

With fingers weary and worn,
With eyelids heavy and red,
A woman sat in unwomanly rags,
   Plying her needle and thread —
                  Stitch! stitch! stitch!
   In poverty, hunger and dirt,
And still with a voice of dolorous pitch, —
Would that its tone could reach the Rich! —
She sang this 'Song of the Shirt'!

The Seal of Robert Bruce.

Scots, wha hae wi' Wallace Bled

(The Address of King Robert Bruce to his Troops before the Battle of Bannockburn)

Robert Burns

Scots, wha hae wi' Wallace bled,
Scots, wham Bruce has aften led;
Welcome to your gory bed,
Or to victorie!

Now's the day, and now's the hour;
See the front of battle lour;
See approach proud Edward's power—
Chains and slaverie!

Wha will be a traitor knave?
Wha can fill a coward's grave?
Wha sae base as be a slave?
Let him turn and flee!

Wha for Scotland's King and Law
Freedom's sword will strongly draw,
Free-man stand, or free-man fa'?
Let him on wi' me!

By oppression's woes and pains!
By your sons in servile chains!
We will drain our dearest veins,
But they shall be free!

Lay the proud usurpers low!
Tyrants fall in every foe!
Liberty's in every blow!
Let us Do, or Die!

71

"...the soldier knew someone had blundered."

The Charge Of The Light Brigade

Lord Tennyson

Half a league, half a league,
Half a league onward,
All in the Valley of Death
Rode the six hundred.
"Forward, the Light Brigade!
Charge for the guns!"he said:
Into the Valley of Death
Rode the Six Hundred.

"Forward, the Light Brigade!"
Was there a man dismayed?
Not tho' the soldier knew
Some one had blundered:
Their's not to make reply,
Their's not to reason why,
Their's but to do and die:
Into the Valley of Death
Rode the Six Hundred.
Cannon to right of them
Cannon to left of them,
Cannon in front of them
Volley'd and thunder'd;
Storm'd at with shot and shell,
Boldly they rode and well,
Into the jaws of Death,
Into the mouth of Hell
Rode the Six Hundred.

Flash'd all their sabres bare,
Flash'd as they turn'd in air
Sabring the gunners there,
Charging an army, while
All the world wonder'd:
Plunged in the battery-smoke
Right thro' the line they broke;
Cossack and Russian
Reel'd from the sabre-stroke
Shatter'd and sunder'd.
Then they rode back, but not—
Not the Six Hundred.

Cannon to right of them,
Cannon to left of them,
Cannon behind them
Volley'd and thunder'd;
Storm'd at with shot and shell
While horse and hero fell,
They that had fought so well
Came thro' the jaws of Death,
Back from the mouth of Hell,
All that was left of them,
Left of Six Hundred.

When can their glory fade?
O the wild charge they made!
All the world wonder'd.
Honour the charge they made!
Honour the Light Brigade,
Noble Six Hundred!

MANDALAY

Rudyard Kipling

By the old Moulmein Pagoda, lookin' lazy at the sea,
There's a Burma girl a-settin', and I know she thinks o' me;
For the wind is in the palm-trees, and the temple-bells they say:
"Come you back, you British soldier; come you back to
Mandalay!"
Come you back to Mandalay,
Where the old Flotilla lay:
Can't you 'ear their paddles chunkin' from Rangoon to Mandalay?
On the road to Mandalay,
Where the flyin'-fishes play,
An' the dawn comes up like thunder out o' China 'crost the Bay!

'Er petticoat was yaller an' 'er little cap was green,
An' 'er name was Supi-yaw-lat—jes' the same as Theebaw's
Queen,
An' I seed her first a-smokin' of a whackin' white cheroot,
An' a-wastin' Christian kisses on an 'eathen idol's foot:
Bloomin' idol made o' mud—
Wot they called the Great Gawd Budd—
Plucky lot she cared for idols when I kissed 'er where she stood!
On the road to Mandalay........

When the mist was on the rice-fields an' and the sun was droppin'
    slow,
She'd git 'er little banjo an' she'd sing *"Kulla-lo-lo!"*
With 'er arm upon my shoulder an' 'er cheek agin my cheek
We useter watch the steamers an' *hathis* pilin' teak.
          Elephants a-pilin' teak
          In the sludgy, squdgy creek,
Where the silence 'ung that 'eavy you was 'arf afraid to speak!
          On the road to Mandalay..........

But that's all shove be'ind me— long ago an' fur away,
An' there ain't no 'buses runnin' from the Bank to Mandalay;
An' I'm learnin' 'ere in London what the ten-year soldier tells:
"If you've 'eard the East a-callin', you won't never 'eed naught
    else."
          No! you won't 'eed nothin' else
          But them spicy garlic smells,
An' the sunshine an' the palm-trees an' the tinkly temple-bells;
          On the road to Mandalay........

I am sick o' wastin' leather on these gritty pavin'-stones,
An' the blasted English drizzle wakes the fever in my bones;
Tho' I walks with fifty 'ousemaids out 'o Chelsea to the Strand,
An' they talks a lot o' lovin' but wot do they understand?
      Beefy face an' grubby 'and—
      Law! wot do they understand?
  I've a neater, sweeter maiden in a cleaner, greener land!
      On the road to Mandalay.........

Ship me somewheres east of Suez, where the best is like the worst,
Where there aren't no Ten Commandments, an' a man can raise a
     thirst;
For the temple-bells are callin' an' it's there that I would be—
By the old Moulmein Pagoda, lookin' lazy at the sea;
      On the road to Mandalay,
      Where the old Flotilla lay,
With our sick beneath the awnings when we went to Mandalay!
      O, the road to Mandalay,
      Where the flyin'-fishes play,
An' the dawn comes up like thunder out 'o China 'crost the Bay!

EXCELSIOR

Henry Wadsworth Longfellow

The shades of night were falling fast,
As through an Alpine village passed
A youth, who bore, 'mid snow and ice,
A banner with the strange device,
        EXCELSIOR!

His brow was sad: his eye beneath
Flashed like a falchion from its sheath,
And like a silver clarion rung
The accents of that unknown tongue,
        EXCELSIOR!

In happy homes he saw the light
Of household fires gleam warm and bright:
Above, the spectral glaciers shone,
And from his lips escaped a groan,
        EXCELSIOR!

"Try not the Pass!"the old man said;
"Dark lowers the tempest overhead,
The roaring torrent is deep and wide!"
And loud that clarion voice replied:
        EXCELSIOR

"O stay," the maiden said, "and rest
Thy weary head upon this breast!"
A tear stood in his bright blue eye,
But still he answered with a sigh,
    EXCELSIOR!

"Beware the pine-tree's withered branch!
Beware the awful avalanche!"
This was the peasant's last Goodnight,
A voice replied, far up the height,
    EXCELSIOR!

At break of day, as heavenward
The pious monks of Saint Bernard
Uttered the oft-repeated prayer,
A voice cried through the startled air,
    EXCELSIOR!

A traveller, by the faithful hound,
Half-buried in the snow was found,
Still grasping in his hand of ice,
That banner with the strange device,
    EXCELSIOR!

There in the twilight cold and gray,
Lifeless, but beautiful, he lay,
And from the sky, serene and far,
A voice fell, like a falling star,

EXCELSIOR!

(Another poet, [it was A.E. Housman, actually,] mocking,
cynically wrote:—)

The shades of night were falling fast,
As through an Alpine village passed
An Alpine village pastor.

79

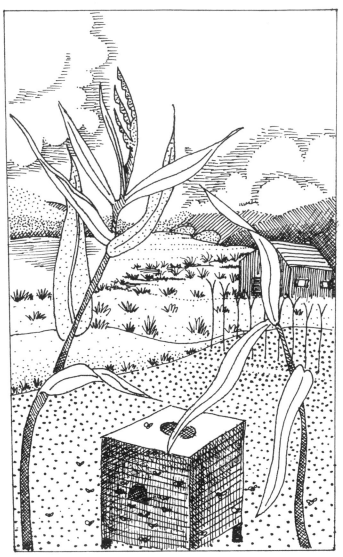

"And I shall have some peace there, for peace comes dropping slow."

The Lake Isle Of Innisfree

William Butler Yeats

I will arise and go now, and go to Innisfree,
And a small cabin build there, of clay and wattles made:
Nine bean-rows will I have there, a hive for the honey-bee,
And live alone in the bee-loud glade.

And I shall have some peace there, for peace comes dropping slow,
Dropping from the veils of the morning to where the cricket sings;
There midnight's all aglimmer, and noon a purple glow,
And evening full of the linnets' wings.

I will arise and go now, for always night and day
I hear lake water lapping with low sounds by the shore;
While I stand on the roadway, or on the pavements grey,
I hear it in the deep heart's core.

The Lost Leader

Robert Browning

Just for a handful of silver he left us,
   Just for a riband to stick in his coat—
Found the one gift of which fortune bereft us,
   Lost all the others she lets us devote;
They, with the gold to give, doled him out silver,
   So much was theirs who so little allowed:
How all our copper had gone for his service!
   Rags—were they purple, his heart had been proud!
We that had loved him so, followed him, honoured him,
   Lived in his mild and magnificent eye,
Learned his great language, caught his clear accents,
   Made him our pattern to live and to die!
Shakespeare was of us, Milton was for us,
   Burns, Shelley, were with us,—they watch from their graves!
He alone breaks from the van and the freemen,
   —He alone sinks to the rear and the slaves!

We shall march prospering,—not through his presence;
   Songs may inspire us,—not from his lyre;
Deeds will be done,—while he boasts his quiescence,
   Still bidding crouch whom the rest bade aspire:
Blot out his name, then, record one lost soul more,
   One task more declined, one more foot-path untrod,
One more devil's triumph and sorrow for angels,
   One more wrong to man, one more insult to God!
Life's night begins: let him never come back to us!
   There would be doubt, hesitation and pain,
Forced praise on our part—the glimmer of twilight,
   Never glad confident morning again!
Best fight on well, for we taught him—strike gallantly,
   Menace our heart ere we master his own;
Then let him receive the new knowledge and wait us
   Pardoned in heaven, the first by the throne!

★ ★ ★ ★ ★

IF——

Rudyard Kipling

If you can keep your head when all about you
    Are losing theirs and blaming it on you,
If you can trust yourself when all men doubt you,
    But make allowance for their doubting too;
If you can wait and not be tired by waiting,
    Or being lied about, don't deal in lies,
Or being hated, don't give way to hating,
    And yet don't look too good, nor talk too wise:

If you can dream—and not make dreams your master;
    If you can think—and not make thoughts your aim;
If you can meet with Triumph and Disaster
    And treat those two imposters just the same;
If you can bear to hear the truth you've spoken
    Twisted by knaves to make a trap for fools,
Or watch the things you gave your life to, broken,
    And stoop and build 'em up with worn-out tools:

If you can make one heap of all your winnings
    And risk it on one turn of pitch-and-toss,
And lose, and start again at your beginnings
    And never breathe a word about your loss;
If you can force your heart and nerve and sinew
    To serve your turn long after they are gone,
And so hold on when there is nothing in you
    Except the Will which says to them: "Hold on!"

If you can talk with crowds and keep your virtue,
    Or walk with Kings—nor lose the common touch,
If neither foes nor loving friends can hurt you,
    If all men count with you, but none too much;
If you can fill the unforgiving minute
    With sixty seconds' worth of distance run,
Yours is the Earth and everything that's in it,
    And—which is more—you'll be a Man, my son!

★★★★★

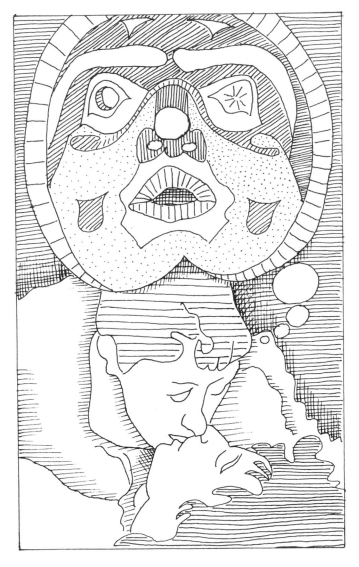

"And the Colonel's daughter smiled on him as well."

THE GREEN EYE
OF THE
LITTLE YELLOW GOD

J. Milton Hayes

There's a little yellow idol to the north of Khatmandu,
There's a little marble cross below the town;
There's a broken-hearted woman tends the grave of Mad
    Carew,
And the Yellow God forever gazes down.

He was known as 'Mad Carew' by the subs. at Khatmandu,
He was hotter than they felt inclined to tell;
But for all his foolish pranks, he was worshipped in the
    ranks,
And the Colonel's daughter smiled on him as well.

He had loved her all along, with a passion of the strong,
The fact that she loved him was plain to all.
She was nearly twenty-one and arrangements had begun
To celebrate her birthday with a ball.

He wrote to ask what present she would like from Mad Carew;
They met next day as he dismissed a squad;
And jestingly she told him then that nothing else would do
But the green eye of the little Yellow God.

On the night before the dance, Mad Carew seemed in a trance,
And they chaffed him as they puffed at their cigars;
But for once he failed to smile, and he sat alone awhile,
Then went out into the night beneath the stars.

He returned before the dawn, with his shirt and tunic torn,
And a gash across his temple dripping red;
He was patched up right away, and he slept through all the day,
And the Colonel's daughter watched beside his bed.

He woke at last and asked if they could send his tunic through;
She brought it, and he thanked her with a nod;
He bade her search the pocket saying "That's from Mad Carew",
And she found the little green eye of the God.

She upbraided poor Carew in the way that women do,
Though both her eyes were strangely hot and wet;
But she wouldn't take the stone, and Mad Carew was left alone
With the jewel that he'd chanced his life to get.

When the ball was at its height, on that still and tropic night,
She thought of him and hastened to his room;
As she crossed the barrack square she could hear the dreamy air
Of a waltz tune softly stealing thro' the gloom.

His door was open wide, with silver moonlight shining through;
The place was wet and slipp'ry where she trod;
An ugly knife lay buried in the heart of Mad Carew,
'Twas the Vengeance of the Little Yellow God.

There's a one-eyed yellow idol to the north of Khatmandu,
There's a little marble cross below the town;
There's a broken-hearted woman tends the grave of Mad Carew,
And the Yellow God forever gazes down.

There's a one-eyed yellow idol to the north of Khatmandu,
There's a little marble cross below the town;
There's a broken-hearted woman tends the grave of Mad Carew,
And the Yellow God forever gazes down.

KUBLA KHAN

Samuel Taylor Coleridge

In Xanadu did Kubla Khan
A stately pleasure-dome decree:
Where Alph, the sacred river, ran
Through caverns measureless to man
Down to a sunless sea.
So twice five miles of fertile ground
With walls and towers were girdled round:
And here were gardens bright with sinuous rills,
Where blossomed many an incense-bearing tree;
And here were forests ancient as the hills,
Enfolding sunny spots of greenery.

But oh! that deep romantic chasm which slanted
Down the green hill athwart a cedarn cover!
A savage place! as holy and enchanted
As e'er beneath a waning moon was haunted
By woman wailing for her demon-lover!
And from this chasm, with ceaseless turmoil seething,
As if this earth in fast thick pants were breathing,
A mighty fountain momently was forced
Amid whose swift half-intermitted burst
Huge fragments vaulted like rebounding hail,
Or chaffy grain beneath the thresher's flail:
And 'mid these dancing rocks at once and ever
It flung up momently the sacred river.
Five miles meandering with a mazy motion
Through wood and vale the sacred river ran,
Then reached the caverns measureless to man,
And sank in tumult to a lifeless ocean:
And 'mid this tumult Kubla heard from far
Ancestral voices prophesying war!

The shadow of the dome of pleasure
Floated midway on the waves;
Where was heard the mingled measure
From the fountain and the caves.
It was a miracle of rare device,
A sunny pleasure-dome with caves of ice!

A damsel with a dulcimer
In a vision once I saw:
It was an Abyssinian maid,
And on her dulcimer she played,
Singing of Mount Abora.
Could I revive within me
Her symphony and song,
To such a deep delight 'twould win me,
That with music loud and long,
I would build that dome in air,
That sunny dome! those caves of ice!
And all who heard should see them there,
And all should cry, "Beware! Beware!
His flashing eyes, his floating hair!
Weave a circle round him thrice,
And close your eyes with holy dread,
For he on honey-dew hath fed,
And drunk the milk of Paradise."

THE WAR SONG OF DINAS FAWR

Thomas Love Peacock

The mountain sheep are sweeter,
But the valley sheep are fatter;
We therefore deemed it meeter
To carry off the latter.
We made an expedition;
We met a host, and quelled it;
We forced a strong position,
And killed the men who held it.

On Dyfed's richest valley,
Where herds of kine were browsing,
We made a mighty sally,
To furnish our carousing.
Fierce warriors rushed to meet us;
We met them, and o'erthrew them:
They struggled hard to beat us;
But we conquered them, and slew them.

As we drove our prize at leisure,
The king marched forth to catch us:
His rage surpassed all measure,
But his people could not match us.
He fled to his hall-pillars;
And, ere our force we led off,
Some sacked his house and cellars,
While others cut his head off.

We there, in strife bewildering,
Spilt blood enough to swim in:
We orphaned many children,
And widowed many women.
The eagles and the ravens
We glutted with our foemen:
The heroes and the cravens,
The spearmen and the bowmen.

We brought away from battle,
And much their land bemoaned them,
Two thousand head of cattle,
And the head of him who owned them:
Ednyfed, King of Dyfed,
His head was borne before us:
His wine and beasts supplied our feasts,
And his overthrow, our chorus.

Flowers Of The Forest
(A Lament for Flodden)

Jane Elliot

I've heard them lilting at our ewe-milking,
  Lasses a-lilting before dawn o' day;
But now they are moaning on ilka green loaning:
  The flowers of the forest are a' wede away.

At bughts, in the morning, nae blythe lads are scorning,
  Lassies are lonely and dowie and wae;
Nae daffing, nae gabbing, but sighing and sabbing.
  Ilk ane lifts her leglin and hies her away.

In hairst, at the shearing, nae youths now are jeering,
  Bandsters are lyart, and runkled and gray;
At fair or at preaching, nae wooing, nae fleeching:
  The flowers of the forest are a' wede away.

At e'en, in the gloaming, nae swankies are roaming,
  'Bout stacks wi' the lasses at bogle to play;
But ilk ane sits eerie, lamenting her dearie:
  The flowers of the forest are a' wede away.

Dool and wae for the order sent our lads to the Border!
  The English, for ance, by guile wan the day;
The flowers of the forest, that fought aye the foremost,
  The prime of our lads, lie cauld in the clay.

We'll hear nae mair lilting at our ewe-milking;
  Women and bairns are heartless and wae;
Sighing and moaning on ilka green loaning:
  The flowers of the forest are a' wede away.

91

"More than two thousand years it is since she was beautiful."

DEIRDRE

James Stephens

Do not let any woman read this verse!
It is for men, and after them their sons,
And their sons' sons!

The time comes when our hearts sink utterly;
When we remember Deirdre and her tale,
And that her lips are dust.

Once she did tread the earth: men took her hand;
They looked into her eyes and said their say,
And she replied to them.

More than two thousand years it is since she
Was beautiful: she trod the waving grass;
She saw the clouds.

Two thousand years!   The grass is still the same;
The clouds as lovely as they were that time
When Deirdre was alive.

But there has been again no woman born
Who was so beautiful; not one so beautiful
Of all the women born.

Let all men go apart and mourn together!
No man can ever love her!   Not a man
Can dream to be her lover!

No man can bend before her!   No man say—
What could one say to her?   There are no words
That one could say to her!

Now she is but a story that is told
Beside the fire!   No man can ever be
The friend of that poor queen!

The War Song Of The Saracens

James Elroy Flecker

We are they who come faster than fate: we are they who ride early or late:
We storm at your ivory gate: Pale Kings of the Sunset beware!
Not in silk nor in samet we lie, not in curtained solemnity die
Among women who chatter and cry and children who mumble a prayer.
But we sleep by the ropes of the camp, and we rise with a shout and we tramp
With the sun or the moon for a lamp, and the spray of the wind in our hair.

From the lands where the elephants are to the forts of Merou and Balghar,
Our steel we have brought and our star to shine on the ruins of Rum.
We have marched from the Indus to Spain, and by God we will go there again;
We have stood on the shore of the plain where the Waters of Destiny boom.
A mart of destruction we made at Jalula where men were afraid,
For death was a difficult trade, and the sword was a broker of doom;
And the Spear was a Desert Physican, who cured not a few of ambition,
And drave not a few to perdition with medicine bitter and strong.

And the shield was a grief to the fool and as bright as a desolate pool,
And as straight as the rock of Stamboul when their cavalry thundered along:
For the coward was drowned with the brave when our battle sheered up like a wave,
And the dead to the desert we gave, and the glory to God in our song.

95

Gunga Din

Rudyard Kipling

You may talk o' gin and beer
When you're quartered safe out 'ere,
An' you're sent to penny-fights an' Aldershot it;
But when it comes to slaughter
You will do your work on water,
An' you'll lick the bloomin' boots of 'im that's got it.
Now in Injia's sunny clime,
Where I used to spend my time
A-servin' of 'Er Majesty the Queen,
Of all them black-faced crew
The finest man I knew
Was our regimental *bhisti*, Gunga Din.
He was "Din! Din! Din!
You limpin' lump o' brick-dust, Gunga Din!
Hi! Slippy *hitherao!*
Water, get it! *Panee lao!*
You squidgy-nosed old idol, Gunga Din."

The uniform 'e wore
Was nothin' much before,
An' rather less than 'arf o' that be'ind,
For a piece 'o twisty rag
An' a goatskin water bag
Was all the field equipment 'e could find.
When the sweatin' troop train lay
In a sidin' through the day,
Where the 'eat would make your bloomin' eyebrows crawl,
We shouted *"Harry By!"*
Till our throats were bricky-dry,
Then we wopped 'im 'cause 'e couldn't serve us all.
It was "Din! Din! Din!
You 'eathen, where the mischief 'ave you been?
You put some *juldee* in it
Or I'll *marrow* you this minute
If you don't fill up my helmet, Gunga Din!"

'E would dot an' carry one
Till the longest day was done;
An' 'e didn't seem to know the use o' fear.
If we charged or broke or cut
You could bet your bloomin' nut,
'E'd be waitin' fifty paces right flank rear.
With 'is *mussick* on 'is back,
'E would skip with our attack,
An' watch us till the bugles made "Retire"
An' for all 'is dirty 'ide,
'E was white, clear white, inside
When 'e went to tend the wounded under fire!
It was "Din! Din! Din!"
With the bullets kickin' dust spots on the green
When the cartridges ran out,
You could 'ear the front ranks shout,
"Hi! Ammunition mules an' Gunga Din!"

97

I sh'n't forget the night
When I dropped be'ind the fight
With a bullet where my belt plate should 'a' been.
I was chokin' mad with thirst,
An' the man that spied me first
Was our good old grinnin' gruntin' Gunga Din.
'E lifted up my 'ead,
An' he plugged me where I bled,
An' 'e gave me 'arf-a-pint o' water green.
It was crawlin' and it stunk,
But of all the drinks I've drunk,
I'm gratefulest to one from Gunga Din.
It was "Din! Din! Din!
'Ere's a beggar with a bullet through 'is spleen;
'E's chawin' up the ground,
An' 'e's kickin' all around:
For Gawd's sake git the water, Gunga Din!"

'E carried me away
to where a *dooli* lay,
An' a bullet came an' drilled the beggar clean.
'E put me safe inside,
An' just before 'e died.
"I 'ope you liked your drink," sez Gunga Din.
So I'll meet 'im later on
At the place were 'e is gone—
Where its always double drill and no canteen.
'E'll be squattin' on the coals
Givin' drink to poor damned souls,
An' I'll get a swig in hell from Gunga Din!
Yes, Din! Din! Din!
You Lazarushian-leather Gunga Din!
Though I've belted you and flayed you,
By the livin' Gawd that made you,
You're a better man I am, Gunga Din!

98

"My name is Ozymandias, King of Kings."

Ozymandias Of Egypt

P.B. Shelley

I met a traveller from an antique land
Who said: Two vast and trunkless legs of stone
Stand in the desert.   Near them on the sand
Half sunk, a shatter'd visage lies, whose frown
And wrinkled lip and sneer of cold command
Tell that its sculptor well those passions read
Which yet survive, stamp'd on these lifeless things,
The hand that mock'd them and the heart that fed:
And on the pedestal these words appear:
"My name is Ozymandias, king of kings:
Look on my works, ye Mighty, and despair!"
Nothing beside remains.   Round the decay
Of that colossal wreck, boundless and bare,
The lone and level sands stretch far away.

Eskimo Nell

Anon.

When a man grows old and his balls grow cold and the end of
    his nob turns blue,
When it's bent in the middle like a one-string fiddle, he can tell
    a tale or two.

So find me a seat and buy me a drink, and a tale to you I'll tell,
Of Dead-Eye Dick and Mexico Pete, and the gentle Eskimo Nell.

When Dead-Eye Dick and Mexico Pete set out in search of fun,
It's Dead-Eye Dick who wields the prick and Mexico Pete the gun.

But when Dead-Eye Dick and the greaser runt are sore, distressed
    and sad,
It's mostly cunt that bears the brunt—though the shootin' ain't
    too bad.

Now Dead-Eye Dick and Mexico Pete had been hunting in
    Deadman's Creek,
And they'd had no luck in the way of a fuck for nigh on half a week,

Just a moose or two, and a caribou, and a buffalo cow or so,
And for Dead-Eye Dick, with his kingly prick, such fucking
    was mighty slow.

So do or dare this horny pair set out for the Rio Grande,
Dead-Eye with swinging prick and Pete with gun in hand.

And thus they blazed their randy trail, and none their fire
withstood,
And many a bride who was hubby's pride knew pregnant widow-
hood.

They made the strand of the Rio Grande at the height of a
blazing noon,
And to slake their thirst and do their worst they sought Black
Mike's saloon.

As the swing doors opened wide, both prick and gun flashed free,
"Accordin' to sex, you bleedin' wrecks, you drinks or fucks
with me."

Now they'd heard of the prick called Dead-Eye Dick from the
Horn to Panama,
So with little worse than a muttered curse those dagoes lined
the bar.

The women too knew his playful ways down on the Rio Grande,
So forty whores tore down their drawers at Dead-Eye Dick's
command.

They saw the fingers of Mexico Pete twitch on the trigger grip,
'Twas death to wait—at a fearful rate those whores began to strip.

Now Dead-Eye Dick was breathing quick with lecherous snorts
and grunts,
As forty arses were bared to view, to say nothing of forty cunts.

Now forty arses and forty cunts you'll see, if you use your wits,
And rattle a bit at arithmetic—that's likewise eighty tits.

And eighty tits is a gladsome sight for a man with a raging stand.
It may be rare in Berkeley Square but not on the Rio Grande.

Our Dead-Eye Dick, he fuck's 'em quick, so he backed and took a
    run,
He took a jump at the nearest rump, and scored a hole in one.

He bore her to the sandy floor and fucked her deep and fine,
And though she grinned, it put the wind up the other thirty-nine.

For when Dead-Eye Dick performs the trick, there's scarcely time
    to spare.
For with speed and strength, on top of length, he fairly singes hair.

Our Dead-Eye Dick he fucks 'em quick, and flinging the first aside,
He made a dart at the second tart, when the swing doors opened
    wide.

And into that hall of sin and vice—into that harlot's hell,
Strode a gentle maid who was unafraid, and her name was Eskimo
    Nell.

Now Dead-Eye Dick had got his prick well into number two,
When Eskimo Nell let out a yell, and called to him "Hi, you!"

The hefty lout he turned about, both nob and face were red,
With a single flick of his mighty prick the tart flew over his head.

But Eskimo Nell she stood it well, and she looked him in the eyes,
With the utmost scorn she looked at the horn that rose from his
    hairy thighs.

"Then at last she stood in her womanhood"

She stubbed out the butt of her cigarette on the end of his gleaming knob,
And so utterly beat was Mexico Pete he forgot to do his job.

It was Eskimo Nell who was first to speak, in accents calm and cool,
"You cuntstruck shrimp of a Yankee pimp, do you call that thing a tool?"

"If this here town can't take that down," she sneered at the cowering whores,
"Here's one little cunt that can do the stunt; it's Eskimo Nell's, not yours!"

She shed her garments one by one with an air of conscious pride,
Till at last she stood in her womanhood, and they saw The Great Divide.

'Tis fair to state, 'twas not so great, though its strength lay well within,
And a better word, that's often heard, would not be *cunt* but *quim*.

She laid right down on the table top where someone had left a glass,
With a flick of her tits she ground it to bits between the cheeks of her arse.

She bent her knees with supple ease and opened her legs apart;
With a smiling nod to the randy sod she gave him the cue to start.

But Dead-Eye Dick with his king of a prick prepared to take his time,
For a Miss like this was perfect bliss, so he staged a pantomime.

He flicked his foreskin up and down, he made his balls inflate,
Until they looked like two granite knobs upon a garden gate.

He winked his arsehole in and out, and his balls increased in size;
His mighty prick grew twice as thick and almost reached his eyes.

He polished it well with alcohol to get it steaming hot,
And to finish the job he sprinkled the knob with the cayenne pepper
     pot.

He didn't back to take a run, nor make a flying leap;
But bent right down and came 'longside with a steady forward
     creep.

Then he took a sight as a gunman might along his mighty tool,
And the long slow glide as it slid inside was firm, calculating and
     cool.

Have you seen the massive pistons on the giant C.P.R.?
With the driving force of a thousand horse—but you know what
     pistons are.

Or you think you do, if you've yet to view the power that drives the
     prick,
Or the work that's done on a non-stop run by a man like Dead-Eye
     Dick.

None but a fool would challenge his tool, no thinking man would
     doubt,
For his fame increased as the Great High Priest of the ceaseless in-
     and-out.

But Eskimo Nell was an infidel, and equalled a whole harem,
With the strength of ten in her abdomen and her Rock of Ages
     beam.

Amidships she could stand the rush like the flush of a water-closet,
So she grasped his cock like the Chatwood lock on the National
 Safe Deposit.

But Dead-Eye Dick would not come quick; he meant to conserve
 his powers,
When in the mind he'd grind and grind for more than a couple of
 hours.

She lay for a while with a subtle smile while the grip of her cunt
 grew keener,
Then giving a sigh she sucked him dry with the ease of a vacuum
 cleaner.

She performed this feat in a way so neat as to set at complete
 defiance
The primary cause and the basic laws that govern sexual science.

She calmly rode through the Phallic Code which for years had
 stood the test,
And the ancient laws of the Classic School in a moment or two
 went west!

And now, my friend, we come to the end of this copulative epic,
For the effect on Dick was sudden and quick and akin to an
 anaesthetic.

He slid to the floor, and he knew no more—his passions extinct and
 dead.
He didn't shout as his tool came out, though 'tis said she'd
 strippped his thread.

Mexico Pete, he sprang to his feet, to avenge his friend's affront,
And his hard-nosed Colt, with a fearful jolt, he rammed right up her
 cunt.

He shoved it hard to the trigger guard, and fired it three times three,
But to his surprise she rolled her eyes and smiled in ecstasy.

She leaped to her feet, with a smile so sweet: "Bully,"she cried,
    "for you;
Though I might have guessed it's about the best that you poor sods
    could do.

"When next, my friend, you two intend to sally forth for fun,
Get Dead-Eye Dick a sugar stick, and buy yourself a bun.

"For I'm away to the frozen North, where pricks are big and strong,
Back to the land of the frozen stand, where the nights are six
    months long.

"When you stick it in, it's as hard as sin, in a land where spunk *is*
    spunk,
Not a trickling stream of lukewarm cream, but a solid frozen chunk.

"Back to the land where they understand what it means to copulate,
Where even the dead lie two in a bed and the infants masturbate.

"They'll tell this tale on the Arctic trail where the nights are sixty
    below,
Where its so damned cold, French letters are sold wrapped in a ball
    of snow.

"Back once more to the sons of men, to the Land of the Midnight
    Sun,
I go to spend a worthy end, for the North is calling '*Come!*'"